THE
GOVERNING
BOARD

Key Responsibilities for Association Boards and Board Members

NANCY R. AXELROD

asae
association
management
press®

WASHINGTON, DC

The author has worked diligently to ensure that all information in this book is accurate as of the time of publication and consistent with standards of good practice in the general management community. As research and practice advance, however, standards may change. For this reason it is recommended that readers evaluate the applicability of any recommendations in light of particular situations and changing standards.

ASAE: The Center for Association Leadership
1575 I Street, NW
Washington, DC 20005-1103
Phone: (202) 626-2723; (888) 950-2723 outside metropolitan Washington, DC area
Fax: (202) 220-6439
Email: books@asaecenter.org

We connect great ideas and great people to inspire leadership and achievement in the association community.

Keith C. Skillman, CAE, Vice President, Publications, ASAE: The Center for Association Leadership
Baron Williams, CAE, Director of Book Publishing, ASAE: The Center for Association Leadership

Cover by Stephen Wilkes
Interior design by Troy Scott Parker, Cimarron Design

This book is available at a special discount when ordered in bulk quantities. For information, contact the ASAE Member Service Center at (202) 371-0940. A complete catalog of titles is available on the ASAE website at www.asaecenter.org.

ISBN-13: 978-0-88034-364-0
ISBN-10: 0-88034-364-8

Printed in the United States of America.

10 9 8 7 6 5 4 3 2 1

CONTENTS

ACKNOWLEDGEMENTS

The author and ASAE would like to express their sincere appreciation to the following individuals for reviewing the manuscript.

- **Lew Gedansky,** Former Director of Governance and Executive Programs, Project Management Institute

- **Arlene Pietranton,** Chief Executive Officer, American Speech-Language-Hearing Association

INTRODUCTION

"A board is a terrible thing to waste."

As a board member, you are in a unique position to make an invaluable contribution to the effectiveness of your board, the performance of your association, and the well-being of your profession or industry. The experience and commitment you bring to the boardroom, however, are not sufficient for successful service. Your board is more likely to become the asset it could be, and should be, if you comprehend your board's collective roles and your responsibilities as an individual board member.

Although boards have always been held accountable for the welfare of their organizations, the climate in which all boards operate is changing. The drivers of change in the association, profession, and industry you serve have underscored your board's role in setting and adjusting your association's course. Boards in all sectors are also subject to a higher level of scrutiny to ensure legal and ethical integrity. Have you noticed how the public greets widely publicized scandals and allegations of impropriety— regardless of the transgression—with the lament of "Where was the board?" Congress, the IRS, state agencies, and the media, along with your association's members, have become far more interested in what goes on in the boardroom.

Your board service requires more than good will, common sense, and good intentions. To help you play a meaningful part in your association's success, this installment in ASAE's Busy Board Series focuses on the primary roles of the association board, your responsibilities as an individual board member, the key characteristics of exceptional boards, and practical ways you and your colleagues can help your board be great.

What's Special About an Association Board?

EACH BOARD IS INFLUENCED by the size, scope, leadership variables, and developmental stage of the organization it governs. Although you're expected to fulfill roles and responsibilities similar to those of other nonprofit board members, serving on an association board means you'll encounter some distinctive traditions and expectations. It's important to understand how these expectations may differ from those you've experienced in the past on the board of another type of organization.

Four key differences affect your board's performance and your behavior as a board member in the association world.

1. **Board composition:** If you're like most association board members, you come from the professional discipline or industry the association serves. This means you and your board colleagues have considerable mission-related professional expertise and experience to contribute. Alas, it can also mean you're more tempted to dive into operational rather than governance matters. This is even more likely if you're moving from a local affiliate to the board of your national or international organization—and especially if you're used to

a board that both manages and governs due to limited or no staff. The transition from a volunteer-driven, hands-on board to a larger, professionally staffed organization can present some board members with a steep learning curve about their appropriate role at an organization with a wider scope.

2. **Board selection:** Most association board members are elected by association members rather than chosen by the board itself, as is typical in the charitable sector. Association members frequently have a limited understanding of the board's role and its work, and relatively few vote in board elections. This places significant responsibility on both your nominating committee and your board to define the competencies—not just the constituencies—your board members need to be effective. These two parties must thoughtfully clarify the qualifications they seek as well as the diversity they value. Otherwise, your association's members are less likely to nominate and elect the most qualified candidates for board service.

3. **Board terms:** At the typical association, approximately one third of the board turns over each year—a significantly higher rate than on other types of boards. This means your board's capacity to work as a high-functioning group is in greater flux as individuals leave and join. The fact that your board chair probably serves a relatively brief one- to two-year term also contributes to continuous change in board composition and dynamics.

4. **Board expectations:** An association board bears responsibility for the financial health of the organization it governs. But unless you serve on the board of either an association foundation or an association established as a charitable organization, you typically will not be expected to solicit funds from individuals, corporations, or foundations. That

said, more organizations of all types are finding it necessary to call on board members to both give money and use their contacts to raise funds for scholarships, research projects, capital campaigns, and more. To be clear about your specific responsibilities, ask your chief elected officer and your chief staff officer what your association expects of you.

Legal Roles and Responsibilities of Individual Board Members and the Collective Board

ALTHOUGH YOU HAVE RESPONSIBILITIES as a board member, you do not have individual authority to make organizational decisions. The board as a whole is responsible for decisions relating to the association regarding, for example, its mission, its strategic plan, its financial condition, its compliance with the law, and its oversight of the chief staff officer. However, the board's shared legal responsibilities depend on the individual actions of you and your fellow board members. Above all, you are expected to act for the good of your organization, not for your own personal benefit or the special interests of the subset of the industry or profession you know so well.

You'll often hear references to the board's fiduciary role, which reflects the board's obligation to protect and enhance the assets of the association. The fiduciary role includes the collective duties of the board as well as the legal obligations of individual board members. These collective and individual duties require each board member to adhere to standards of conduct commonly referred to as "the 3 Ds"—duties you can neither delegate nor abdicate.

The Three Ds:
Legal Duties of the Board and Board Members

Board Duty	Ways in Which You Can Fulfill This Duty
The Duty of Care: The board and the board member's obligation to be reasonably informed, to act in good faith, and to be diligent in making decisions.	• Use your best judgment. • Stay informed about the performance and health of your association. • Prepare for and attend board and committee meetings. • Ask good questions. • Participate in discussions, deliberations, and decisions. • Make decisions based on sound information (including the subject-matter expertise of professionals retained to advise the board) rather than opinions. • Do not disclose confidential information about the association.

Board Duty	Ways in Which You Can Fulfill This Duty
The Duty of Loyalty: The board and the board member's obligation to be accountable by putting your personal interests aside for the greater good of the association.	• Act on behalf of the good of your organization, not your personal or professional interests nor the interests of a special constituency. • Comply with your association's written conflict-of-interest policy regarding disclosure, avoidance, recusal, and management of conflicts of interest. • Make the interests of the association your primary focus and commitment in your board work.
The Duty of Obedience: The board and the board member's obligation to comply with legal, regulatory, and reporting requirements and to serve as a guardian of your association's mission.	• Make decisions that conform to your association's mission. • Comply with applicable federal, state, and local laws (e.g., filing tax forms, paying employment taxes, and publicly disclosing selective information). • Adhere to your organization's bylaws and other governing documents.

A board member may be subject to personal liability if he or she breaches the standards of fiduciary responsibility. This primer's review of your legal responsibilities as an individual board member is no substitute for the advice of trained professionals. Your association's legal counsel should thoroughly explain the three duties during all orientations for new board members and review them with your entire board on a regular basis. This will help ensure that your board has adequate policies and practices to meet its requirements throughout the year and keep up with changes from the IRS, state agencies, and other regulatory bodies.

Key Roles of Association Boards

Y**OUR BOARD SERVES AS** the ultimate steward to ensure that all of your association's assets are protected. The following four overlapping roles underscore the key ways in which your board can add the greatest value. Each section describes both what good boards do and the extra measures better boards take for optimal performance.

1. Set direction.

Good boards know they are ultimately responsible for the association's mission. One of the most important ways your board can advance the mission is by using it as a core driver to set the association's direction and determine priorities. Although your board must govern to meet today's challenges, it must also help your association remain relevant to tomorrow's world. If your board fails to respond to and instigate change when conditions warrant, it is less likely to make timely, constructive decisions that protect the association's viability and future performance.

Better boards, in concert with their management teams, protect their associations' long-term prospects by

- Regularly reviewing the mission to ensure that it continues to serve as a guidepost for everything the association does.

- Establishing strategic goals, identifying strategic priorities, and contributing to critical strategies to achieve those goals.

- Planning for the future, not by attempting to predict it but by positioning the association to be ready for whatever the future brings. As your association faces internal and external changes, your board should monitor its surrounding market, track progress toward key goals, and assess the results of efforts to attain them.

- Organizing the board's structure and agenda to conduct its business in light of the association's strategic priorities.

2. Ensure and protect resources.

One of the ways *good boards* fulfill their fiduciary role is by ensuring that their organizations secure and conserve adequate financial resources. In associations, major sources of revenue include membership dues, fees for programs and services, and investment income.

In addition, boards carry out their fiduciary role by protecting three other critical assets: human resources (e.g., staff, volunteers, and members), physical assets, and the reputation and image of the association.

> "Sustainability encompasses both financial sustainability (the ability to generate resources to meet the needs of the present without compromising the future) and programmatic sustainability (the ability to develop, mature, and cycle out programs to be responsive to constituencies over time)."
> – *Nonprofit Sustainability: Making Strategic Decision for Financial Viability* by Jeanne Bell, Jan Masaoka, and Steve Zimmerman (Jossey-Bass, 2010)

Better boards, with support from the management team, protect resources in a number of important ways, including by

- Ensuring that the association's current revenue sources are stable in the near term and sustainable for the long term.

- Making certain that income is managed properly and financial statements are accurate, intelligible, and timely so that they reflect key financial transactions and the association's true financial condition.

- Taking the time to learn the key financial drivers that generate resources, productivity, and program quality.

- Ensuring that human resources and risk management policies and practices are in place to protect the well-being, safety, and development of staff, volunteers, members, and other key stakeholders.

- Following ethical norms, protecting the association from legal action, and safeguarding the association's integrity and brand.

3. Engage in outreach.

Good boards serve as bridges between the association and its members. Because they're usually members of the association, board members tend to be well equipped to fulfill this relationship-builder role with multiple stakeholders. In some associations, boards are also expected to engage in advocacy work to help shape public policy that advances the profession or industry.

Better boards, in concert with their management teams, fulfill their outreach role by

- Deploying board members as ambassadors who communicate the association's mission and activities to its different constituencies.

- Understanding, interpreting, and communicating the diverse needs and perspectives of the association's members in a manner that will inform the board's decisions.

- Defining the association's position on public policies and serving as advocates when asked to do so.

- Serving as buffers (and even "loving internal critics" when appropriate) to protect the association from intrusions from special interests, regulatory initiatives, or unethical behavior that violate the association's mission or values.

4. Provide oversight.

"Exceptional boards govern in constructive partnership with the chief executive, recognizing that the effectiveness of the board and chief executive are interdependent."
– The Source: Twelve Principles of Governance That Power Exceptional Boards (BoardSource, 2005)

Good boards oversee the assets that have the greatest impact on the association's health and well-being—including the chief staff officer. The board depends, in part, on the chief staff officer (and his or her staff) to provide the information the board needs to govern well; the chief staff officer depends on the board for the authority to lead and manage the association on a day-to-day basis. Problems can arise when these respective roles are unclear, when there are too many overlapping areas in which more than one party has authority, or when individual board members attempt to direct the staff. It all works best when the chief elected officer and chief staff officer understand their shared and distinctive responsibilities to lead and educate the board and are committed to each other's success.

One of the most critical ways in which a board fulfills its oversight role is by selecting and supporting the chief staff officer and then reviewing his or her performance. This board role is advanced by providing regular feedback and a leadership climate in which the chief staff officer can succeed. Boards cannot govern well without the chief staff officer's collaboration, and the chief staff officer is less likely to lead effectively without the unflagging support of the board. By doing these things well, your board can truly hold the chief staff officer accountable. But in case the association ever has to replace a chief staff officer unexpectedly, your board should be sure to have emergency leadership-transition plans in place.

Better boards monitor the association's performance and progress against established goals and priorities as well as critical drivers of change. These boards:

- Focus on what's most important to watch, rather than trying to examine everything.

- Ensure that policies and diagnostic tools are in place to regularly evaluate the association's infrastructure, programs, and services to determine if they advance the mission and serve the association's constituencies.

- Establish nominations and election practices that attract the best and the brightest to board service.

- Provide thorough orientation for new board members and ongoing education for all board members.

- Regularly assess the board's own performance for the purpose of learning and improving.

Three Characteristics
That Distinguish
Great Boards

YOU'RE PROBABLY WELL AWARE that the growing interest in boards has sparked the vigilance of the IRS, Congress, state regulatory bodies, and investigative journalists. It has also motivated boards to govern more diligently and responsively. Board members are requesting clearer governance information, asking better questions, and challenging things that don't seem right. Some boards have changed their meetings to devote more time to tracking emerging trends and ensuring data-driven, outcome-based decisions. Others have reduced the number of permanent standing committees and increased the use of task forces to respond to rapidly changing needs. More boards are making a regular practice of conducting board self-assessments.

And many boards are starting to profile the competencies they need to see in future board members as well as to widen the leadership development pathway for the next generation of association volunteers.

The new perception that good governance is intentional—rather than accidental or incidental—is long overdue. It should not be a news flash to anyone that assembling a group of competent individuals does not automatically create a competent board. Having "the right people on the bus" and providing robust fiduciary oversight are essential—but clearly not adequate—for exceptional governance.

So if a one-size-fits-all, good-governance recipe book doesn't produce good boards, what does? The growing body of governance research (conducted by thoughtful observers from education, healthcare, and the for-profit, charitable, and association sectors) and the lessons learned from high-profile cases of "nongovernance" illuminate salient traits of high-performing boards. Your role will be enhanced if you understand the following three characteristics that consistently emerge to separate the best from the rest.

1. A Culture of Candor, Respect, and Inquiry

> "What distinguishes exemplary boards is that they are robust, effective social systems."
>
> **– Jeffrey A. Sonnenfeld in "What Makes Great Boards Great" in *Harvard Business Review*, 2002.**

On the surface, it appears that many of the companies and nonprofits plagued by well-publicized mismanagement and malfeasance had boards that followed the conventional benchmarks of good governance. But even when there was no evidence of corruption or abuse at the board level, all these cases reflect governance breakdowns. What many of these boards lacked was a culture in which interested, highly engaged board members were encouraged to ask questions and rewarded for constructive debate on vital issues and priorities.

A board's culture encompasses the traditions, written and unwritten rules, beliefs, and norms that predominate when it convenes for its work. Without a robust and well-documented decision-making infrastructure to promote dialogue, debate, and deliberation, it's all too easy for a board to function passively or reactively.

Three unfortunate consequences can arise when your board squelches challenging questions and constructive dissent or when decisions become perfunctory:

- Your board is less likely to make good decisions on high-stakes issues in which views are polarized and emotions run high.

- Your board's desire to avoid conflict can provide a breeding ground for the twin pathologies of dysfunctional politeness and groupthink.

- Some board members are likely to take their differences *outside* the board room to share with others.

The four key enablers of a culture of candor and respect are

- There is a tone of respect and openness at the top (which grows out of the governance climate your chief elected officer and chief staff officer help create).

- The entire board agrees on the optimal norms of behavior for how board members will operate as a group.

- Board members have the opportunity to get to know each other in informal settings, such as meals and board retreats.

- Meetings allot sufficient time for discussion, dialogue, and debate to inform the board's decisions.

MARKERS OF A BOARD CULTURE OF CANDOR AND RESPECT

- A sense of mutual respect, trust, and inclusiveness among board members and between board and staff.

- The capacity to explore divergent views in a respectful (rather than adversarial) manner.

- Constructive (rather than destructive) dissent and debate.

- Willingness to gather relevant information (rather than rely on opinions) to inform decisions.

- Equal access to information.

- Active feedback mechanisms that help the board engage in continuous improvement.

- Individual and collective commitments to decisions, plans of action, and accountability to follow through on the board's agreements.

Adapted with permission from *Culture of Inquiry: Healthy Debate in the Boardroom* by Nancy R. Axelrod, a publication of BoardSource. For more information about BoardSource, call 800-883-6262 or visit www.boardsource.org. BoardSource © 2007. Content may not be reproduced or used for any purpose other than that which is specifically requested without written permission from BoardSource.

2. An Appetite for Continuous Learning and Improvement

Like other institutions and individuals, your board is unlikely to learn and grow without feedback on its performance and opportunities to make continuous improvements. Effective boards allot a time and discipline to self-improvement by inviting board members to periodically assess the board's composition, structure, culture, and overall performance. These boards take steps to make sure board members stay informed about three key domains:

- the work of the association

- critical trends and drivers of change in the industry or profession and the larger societal context in which your

MARKERS OF CONTINUING EDUCATION AND IMPROVEMENT

- An orientation program for your new board members that does not orient all at once by "fire hose."

- Opportunities at each meeting to educate your board about the association, opportunities and threats in your profession or industry, or good governance practice.

- A regular process for your board to assess either a facet of its own membership, structure, or process or its overall performance and effectiveness; and a way for individual board members to review their own performance.

- Social events, informal time, and dedicated forums (such as board retreats) that build your board's social fabric.

- A competency-based board succession plan that guides the nominations process.

- An adequate budget for board education and development.

- A chief staff officer and chief elected officer who willingly invest in governance capacity.

association operates that will have the greatest impact on the members

- the board's roles, board members' responsibilities, and relevant research findings that illuminate best practices in the world of association governance and organizational capacity

Because higher turnover within association boards creates greater change within the team of players each year, your board is more likely to stay effective if the following are true:

- Board development is viewed as an ongoing activity to sustain what works and improve what could be working better.

- Educational activities are hard-wired into board meetings and other forums so that your board can model itself as a learning organization.

- Your board and staff leaders recognize that if they invest scant time in board infrastructure, education, and ongoing development, your association is less likely to have a board that matters.

3. The Capacity to Think and Act Strategically

> "Two of the most important concepts in a leader's toolkit are context and perspective. But it is easy for association leaders to get caught up in responding to the problems of the day and to under-invest in viewing the big picture to be responsive to opportunities and threats. One of the qualities ascribed to star athletes is their capacity to play hard while keeping the whole game enterprise in mind as if they stood on a balcony above the field of play. Like stellar athletes, the best boards try not to get swept up in the daily fray of tactics and immediate problems. Rather, they scan the horizon and calibrate the association's appropriate pace of change for the industry or profession it serves."
>
> *– Governing for Growth: Using 7 Measures of Success to Strengthen Board Dialogue and Decision Making* **by Nancy R. Axelrod (ASAE, 2009)**

The faster, deeper pace of change throughout your profession, industry, and the world calls for you and your fellow board members to play a strategic role as leaders as well as a fiduciary role as stewards. Few would dispute that your board members can offer intellectual and social capital to tackle significant issues facing your association. But don't underestimate the common tendency of some board members to jump into the thicket of operational or less consequential matters that don't warrant the board's time and attention.

The more your board and staff understand why strategic thinking is *not* a natural act for most boards, the higher the probability that you and your fellow board members can surmount the following governance gremlins lurking beneath your boardroom table.

- If your board members are like most others, in your day jobs you're practitioners who are typically rewarded for managing, not experts who are highly knowledgeable about governing. Even if you're a senior leader with a strategic role, you probably aren't expected to work as board members do—sharing equal power with several others and making decisions by consensus.

- Individual board members are often asked to roll up their sleeves and play operational roles such as ambassadors at the same time that the collective board is discouraged from managing rather than governing. This can create ambiguity for some board members in sorting out the appropriate role of the board versus the board member.

- The built-in high turnover rate in your association board makes strategic thinking elusive because new board members typically lack the experience to hit the ground running on board-approved strategic directions, institutional priorities, and governance practices.

As mentioned earlier, many boards lack the bandwidth for strategic thinking. If your board does not possess meaningful information, strategic agendas, and a reliable infrastructure for decision making, it's unrealistic to expect it to operate strategically. Board meetings driven by reports rather than issues discourage strategic thinking. If you're given too little or too much information, this can limit your contribution to strategic issues and outcomes. But all too often, the information prepared for boards and board committees tends to be administrative rather than governance-oriented.

High-performing boards are able to surmount these weaknesses. Their members insist on receiving adequate information to fulfill their responsibilities. They monitor, and if necessary restructure, the board's use of committee and meeting time to emphasize institutional priorities—not administrivia or personal agendas.

MARKERS OF STRATEGIC BOARDS

- Willingness to help shape the association's priorities through the strategic planning process.
- Alignment between the board meeting agenda and the association's goals and priorities.
- Use of a consent agenda (for issues that require board approval but not necessarily discussion) to help the board allot sufficient time to critical issues and robust dialogue and debate.
- High priority placed on addressing long-range strategic issues that confront the association.
- Commitment to anticipate potential problems before issues become urgent.
- Willingness to sharpen direction, address difficult issues, and identify opportunities.
- Ability to react to and interpret data-based information in a manner that leads to clear choices, decisions, and actions.
- The commitment to allocate the board's time to what matters most to the association's performance and future viability.
- Meetings that focus on governing rather than managing.

Envisioning a New Model: How Well Do You Contribute to the *Four-Sighted Board*?

LEADERS HAVE BEEN DEBATING governance models for years. The quest for a better board structure is fueled by the legitimate beef that too few association boards add as much value as they could, and should. But changing your board's structure or composition merely because of dissatisfaction with the status quo is unlikely to yield much return on investment. Trying to build a shiny new board model is futile without two core requirements:

- clarity and consensus on how your board can add the greatest value

- the will to act and make changes to support that value proposition

The majority of governance changes—incremental or radical—enacted during the last few years have been prompted by the clarion call for boards to operate as richer strategic assets rather than "legal necessities" or "sidewalk superintendents." The opportunity costs of the latter two models are significant. You don't have to Google the term "strategic" to know that this three-syllable word is one of the most overused and mind-numbing in the leadership lexicon. For a fresh perspective, give yourself a regular vision exam to test how well you contribute to your board's following *four sights.*

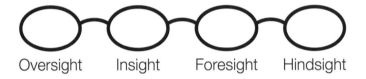

Oversight   Insight   Foresight   Hindsight

Oversight

Your board is legally required to oversee the financial, human, physical, and reputational assets of your association. It accomplishes this task in many ways, such as approving the budget, establishing reliable risk-management mechanisms and internal controls, overseeing the chief staff officer's performance, and monitoring the progress of the strategic plan.

If yours is a successful board, it provides responsible oversight by making sure the association is well run, rather than trying to run the association itself.

Insight

Your board members are uniquely positioned to offer expertise and experience in the profession or industry your association serves. The board can do this in multiple ways, such as sharing insights that will inform the association's services or flagging programs that are candidates for what Peter Drucker labels "purposeful abandonment."

If yours is a successful board, it also provides insight by continually monitoring the association's strategic goals and priorities against desired results and outcome metrics, rather than treating the strategic plan as "credenza-ware."

Foresight

This is one of the most underused board sights. Your board members can add a distinctive core competency by identifying and discussing the impact of emerging issues and trends on your association, its members, and the field it serves.

If yours is a successful board, it does this by allocating sufficient board meeting time to the embryonic issues, disruptive technologies, ambiguous threats, and new opportunities that are most likely to be game-changers in your profession and industry.

Hindsight

Hindsight tends to be dissed as unrealistic because you can only get the benefits of it after the fact. But your board needs to look back in order to move forward properly. Without common agreement on past performance, it's harder for your association leaders to create a shared vision of the future and consensus on priorities.

Crises, like victories, should not be wasted. Your association shouldn't summarily dismiss failures with the easy rhetoric of outrage or blame. If yours is a successful board, it reflects on setbacks and governance breakdowns (as well as successes) that offer the most teachable lessons for future performance.

Good Boards Can Always Be Better

KEEP IN MIND THAT there is at least one constant in the dynamic world of association governance. Whether the board you now serve on is heroic, good enough, or dysfunctional, you can expect it to change—at least annually. Change on your board may be inevitable, but growth is always optional.

Fortunately, a board, like the human brain, is capable of altering its structure and function (and even generating new cells) in response to experience and new information. Your board's governance practices do not have to be broken to be improved. Perhaps the greatest peril for your board is to become complacent and think that, unlike every other aspect of your association's infrastructure, the board itself is not a candidate for continuous learning and improvement.

Although most association leaders yearn for their boards to govern as leaders rather than tacticians, too often they neglect to provide the tools to enhance board members' time and talents. Many board and staff leaders continue to search for new governance *models* to fix underperforming boards: If only you could get the right people or change the board's size, surely it would morph into a strategic board! But your board's capacity to exercise wise stewardship and strategic thinking depends on more than its composition and architecture. It is heavily influenced by its cultural DNA, the way in which board members' precious time is allocated at board and committee meetings, the kind of help it gets to function as a strategic asset, and your behavior.

The good news is that your board can always become better with the help of association leaders who get that "a good board is a victory, not a gift." Whether you serve on or work with your association board, you can make a discernible difference in institutionalizing board development as an ongoing process rather than an intermittent activity. New board models, strategic plans, and best practices are less likely to succeed without your help in building high-performing, highly effective governance.

The Right Work in the Right Way: 10 Tips for Individual Board Members

DOES YOUR BOARD STRUGGLE to define its real work? Do you wish your board had more tools to act and think strategically? Are individual board members micromanaging or under-engaged?

Your chief staff officer and chief elected officer bear primary responsibility—as your association's "chief board development officers"—to help your board do the right work in the right way. But don't underestimate how much you can enhance or impede your board's effectiveness. Now that you have a better understanding of how even a good board can always be better, consider these 10 ways in which you can help make your board great.

1. Use your association's mission statement as a guidepost, and place the interests of the association first in any decisions your board makes.

2. Learn your association's key financial drivers and ask the right questions. For example, instead of focusing on a small line item in the budget submitted to the board for approval, ask how your association's financial plan is aligned with its strategic plan or whether key sources of revenue or expenses are rising or falling.

3. Let your chief elected officer and chief staff officer know what you most need to learn about your association, trends in the profession and industry you serve, or your fiduciary obligations and best practices to fulfill your governance responsibilities.

4. Contribute to your board's culture of candor and inquiry by "athletically listening" (rather than listening to react) to the diverse views of your colleagues; challenging assumptions you might question in a civil, respectful way; and resolving differences inside rather than outside the boardroom.

5. Help your board devote as much time as possible to the issues with the greatest impact on your association's success and vitality. To address those issues, request board meeting materials that will help the board provide insight and foresight, as well as oversight and hindsight.

6. Respect your association's reporting lines and communication channels. Don't supervise, micromanage, or befriend individual staff members, all of whom report either directly or indirectly to the chief staff officer.

7. Focus your time on the responsibilities assigned to the collective board and its individual members, rather than getting enmeshed in the tactics and implementation assigned to staff members or other groups.

8. Participate in the self-improvement process your board uses to assess its performance each year. Periodically ask yourself how well you think you contribute to the board's work and what you can do or might need to be as effective as possible.

9. Help with board succession planning by identifying association members who are good candidates for the pipeline of potential volunteer leaders.

10. Encourage your fellow board members to help the board make data-driven decisions based on information rather than opinions.

FOR FURTHER READING

- *Culture of Inquiry: Healthy Debate in the Boardroom* by Nancy Axelrod (BoardSource, 2007).

- *Governing for Growth: Using 7 Measures of Success to Strengthen Board Dialogue and Decision Making* by Nancy Axelrod (ASAE, 2009); and its companion volume, *Governing for Growth Facilitator's Guide* by Nancy Axelrod (ASAE, 2010).

- *7 Measures of Success: What Remarkable Associations Do That Others Don't, Revised and Updated Edition* (ASAE: The Center for Association Leadership, 2012).

- *The Source: Twelve Principles of Governance That Power Exceptional Boards* (BoardSource, 2005).

- *The Volunteer Leadership Issue,* published every January by the staff of ASAE's *Associations Now* magazine (www.asaecenter.org).

ABOUT THE AUTHOR

Nancy R. Axelrod, a governance consultant based in Washington, DC, is a frequent speaker at conferences and leadership forums dedicated to governance, accountability, and board development. She is the founding president of BoardSource, where she served as its first chief executive officer from 1987 to 1996. She serves on the faculty of "Exceptional Boards: Strengthening the Leadership Team" (an ASAE workshop for teams of board officers and chief executives) and the "Institute for Presidents and Boards Chairs of Independent Colleges and Universities" (sponsored by the Association of Governing Boards of Universities and Colleges).

Axelrod is the author of *Governing for Growth: Using 7 Measures of Success to Strengthen Board Dialogue and Decision Making* and its companion *Governing for Growth Facilitator's Guide; Culture of Inquiry: Healthy Debate in the Boardroom; Advisory Councils; Chief Executive Succession Planning: Essential Guidance for Boards and CEOs;* and numerous articles and op-ed pieces. She has served as a member of a number of governing and advisory boards. You can reach her at www.nancyaxelrod.com.